Pitch In!

Kids Talk About Cooperation

Written by Pamela Hill Nettleton ••• Illustrated by Amy Bailey Muehlenhardt

Thanks to our advisers for their expertise, research, and advice:

Stephanie Goerger Sandahl, M.A., Counseling
Lutheran Social Services of Minnesota
Fergus Falls, Minnesota

Susan Kesselring, M.A., Literacy Educator
Rosemount-Apple Valley-Eagan (Minnesota) School District

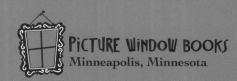

PICTURE WINDOW BOOKS
Minneapolis, Minnesota

Managing Editors: Bob Temple, Catherine Neitge
Creative Director: Terri Foley
Editors: Brenda Haugen, Christianne Jones
Editorial Adviser: Andrea Cascardi
Designer: Nathan Gassman
Page production: Picture Window Books
The illustrations in this book were rendered digitally.

Picture Window Books
5115 Excelsior Boulevard
Suite 232
Minneapolis, MN 55416
877-845-8392
www.picturewindowbooks.com

Printed in the United States of America.

Library of Congress Cataloging-in-Publication Data
Nettleton, Pamela Hill.
Pitch in! : kids talk about cooperation / written by Pamela Hill Nettleton ; illustrated
   by Amy Bailey Muehlenhardt.
p. cm. – (Kids talk)
Includes bibliographical references and index.
ISBN 1-4048-0621-0 (reinforced library binding : alk. paper)
1. Cooperativeness–Miscellaneous–Juvenile literature. I. Muehlenhardt, Amy Bailey,
   1974– II. Title. III. Series.

BJ1533.C74N48 2004
179'.9–dc22   2003028243

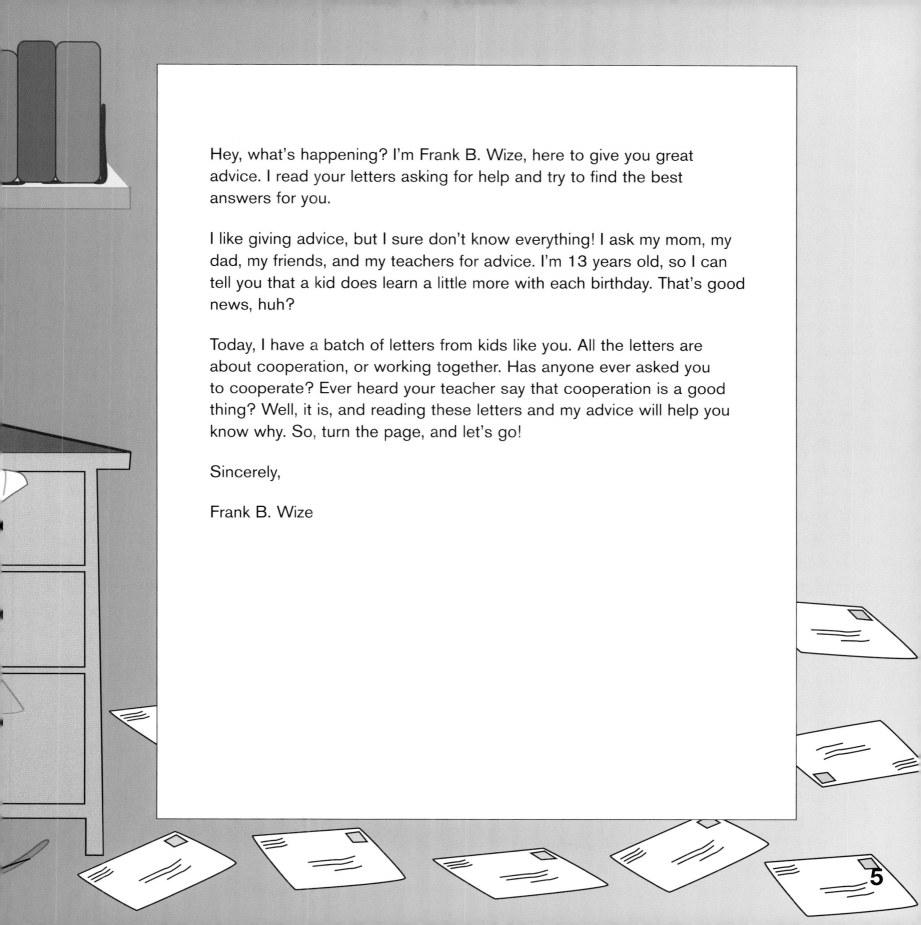

Hey, what's happening? I'm Frank B. Wize, here to give you great advice. I read your letters asking for help and try to find the best answers for you.

I like giving advice, but I sure don't know everything! I ask my mom, my dad, my friends, and my teachers for advice. I'm 13 years old, so I can tell you that a kid does learn a little more with each birthday. That's good news, huh?

Today, I have a batch of letters from kids like you. All the letters are about cooperation, or working together. Has anyone ever asked you to cooperate? Ever heard your teacher say that cooperation is a good thing? Well, it is, and reading these letters and my advice will help you know why. So, turn the page, and let's go!

Sincerely,

Frank B. Wize

Dear Frank,

My sister is on the phone all the time! She talks to her friends. She talks to her friends' friends. She talks to my mom at work. She talks to her friends some more. I think the phone is stuck to her ear with glue!

My friends don't get a chance to talk to me on the phone—even when it's really important! My mom says I'm too young to have a cell phone. I can't think of a way to deal with this!

Myra

Dear Myra,

Your sister's ear must hurt! Seriously, you and your sister have to figure out how to share the phone. That means you have to cooperate, or find a way to work together.

I asked my mom for some ideas. She said you could make a chart of who talks on the phone when. Maybe your sister has the phone from 3 o'clock to 4 o'clock, and you have it from 4 to 5. You can tell all your friends to call during your special time.

My mom also said you could put a kitchen timer by the phone. Each call can only last five minutes. When the timer goes off, the phone call is done. If your sister won't agree, then you need to go to your mom or dad and ask for some help. If you go to them with a plan—like using the timer—they might be more likely to see things your way. At least they'll see you are trying to cooperate!

Frank

Dear Frank,

At school, we are working on small-group projects. My group has four kids. We're supposed to be working together to make a book of poems. We all get the same grade. Our group decided we would each write three poems, but Jeremy hasn't even written one! When we're working together, he just sits there. He won't help at all! Why should Jeremy get a good grade if he doesn't help with any of the work? What can we do?

Ethan

Dear Ethan,

Those small-group projects can be lots of fun if you all pitch in. When you get a kid like Jeremy in your group, trying to work together can be a pain. It doesn't feel fair that Jeremy would get the same grade as everyone else when he didn't help.

I wonder why Jeremy won't write his poems. Maybe you could ask him. Maybe he thinks he's a bad poet. Maybe he's afraid to try because he thinks you'll tease him. Maybe he wasn't paying attention in class, and now he isn't sure how to do it.

Here's an idea. Try asking him what he'd like to do on this project. If Jeremy won't write any poems, maybe he would draw pictures for each of the poems the rest of you wrote. He might have some great ideas.

If Jeremy still doesn't help, talk to your teacher. I'm sure he'll know what to do!

Frank

Dear Frank,

My teacher, Mrs. Baker, is all mad because I was talking to my friend Susie during class. The class is boring, and Susie and I just talked for a minute. What's the big deal? My grade will still be an A.

Marie

Dear Marie,

You might get an A whether or not you listen to your teacher, but there are two things wrong with talking while your teacher is teaching. Two things that have nothing to do with you and your grade.

First, it's really rude to talk while Mrs. Baker is trying to teach. What if you were giving a book report in front of the class and kids in the back row were laughing? It would be tough for you to concentrate and do a good job. That's what it's like for Mrs. Baker when you're talking.

Second, even if you think you'll get a good grade, what about the other kids? Maybe some of your classmates need to listen harder than you do to get a good grade. It might be tough for them to hear over you and Susie talking.

So, shhhhh! You and Susie can talk all you want during recess and after class. In class, try to be considerate and cooperative.

Frank

Dear Frank,

My dad wants me to clean out the garage, but I don't know where most of the stuff goes. What do I do with the broom? Where do I hang the rakes? I want to do a good job, but I don't really know what I'm doing. Where do I start?

Steve

12

Dear Steve,

This sounds like a job that calls for a little cooperation. Let me tell you a story about something like this that happened to me.

My mom asked me to clean my room, but I didn't do it. My room was a big mess. Clothes on the floor, homework in piles on my desk, old soda cans sitting around. I just couldn't figure out where to start. The next time my mom bugged me about my room, I told her I wanted to clean it, but the job was just too big. My mom said we should cooperate.

"I'll do all the planning," she said. "Then you do all the cleaning." She came up to my room and made a list. "Don't think about how big the job is," she told me. "Just work your way down the list. Cross each thing off when you get it done." It totally helped me! I had my room clean in no time.

Go to your dad, and tell him you are happy to clean the garage—but first, you need his help planning. Ask him to make a list for you or to come to the garage and tell you what to do first, second, and third. This is cooperating. You let him know what you are willing to do, but you also let him know where you need his help.

Frank

15

Dear Frank,

There is a vacant lot in our neighborhood. I saw a TV show where some kids made an empty lot into a cool garden. I want to do that in our neighborhood. My mom said I need to find some community partners. What does that mean?

Terese

Dear Terese,

Community means a group of people. The people who live in your city are a community. You also have a school community—all the kids and teachers at school. You might even have a church community—all your friends and their families who go to your church.

Partners are people who will help you with a big job. Turning an empty lot into a garden is a big job. Think of what you will need: garden tools, seeds, fertilizer, people to hoe the garden. That's a lot of stuff for one kid to worry about!

Sounds like your mom thinks your idea is cool. She wants you to find some help in your neighborhood. Let's think. Who could help you? Is there a garden store nearby that might give you some seeds or a few plants? Are there some gardeners on your block? They could help you plant the garden and might even work in it.

You can get way more done when you find people who will cooperate! Good luck, Terese!

Frank

18

Dear Frank,

My stepbrother is a big pain. Now that my dad married my stepmom, I have to go on vacation with Ricky. He is younger than I am, and he never leaves me alone. He makes snorting noises all the time. He spits when he talks. I just know he's gonna bug me all the way to the Grand Canyon. Help!

Alex

Dear Alex,

Here's a news flash: I'll bet Ricky thinks you are really cool. No, really. Remember what you thought of guys your age back when you were a little guy like Ricky? Now you are his cool older brother. That's probably why he sticks to you like glue.

If you guys fight all the way to the Grand Canyon, your parents are going to go nuts—and you'll probably be the guy they yell at. After all, you're the older brother.

Here's a tip for you: Before you leave on vacation, talk to Ricky a few times to find out some things he likes to do in the car. Maybe you could come up with some stuff, too. There's the license plate game, where you try to find license plates from all 50 states and then cross them off on a map. You'll be a hero to Ricky and to your dad and stepmom.

Frank

Dear Frank,

I am in charge of costumes for our school play. The girl who is in charge of music is so mean. She doesn't like any of my ideas. The boy who is the main actor likes my ideas but hates the music. Another boy who makes the scenery wants to do it his way and doesn't care what the rest of us are saying. How can we ever get this play done?

Letty

Dear Letty,

Man, oh man! You guys need a little help! What isn't happening here? Cooperation, our word of the day! Each one of you has your own job to do, but none of you are working together.

My dad runs into these kinds of problems at his office a lot. I'll pass his advice on to you: "You have to find out what you have in common."

What do you and these other kids have in common? Making a great play, for one thing. Each of you wants your costumes and the music, acting, and scenery to be cool. If you're fighting all the time, nothing will look cool.

It's time to get down to business. Call a meeting of all the kids working on the play. Tell everyone the truth—there are lots of cool ideas here, but everyone has to work together. Try going around the table and letting each kid talk about his or her ideas. After everyone has had a chance to speak, ask the group to talk about whether all these ideas make sense together. You might be surprised at the good ideas you hear! Now go break a leg! Not literally, that's just showbiz talk for good luck.

Frank

Dear Frank,

I need some help with math. I am really good at writing, but math is not easy for me. There is a girl in my class who is a math whiz. I'd like her help, but I'm not sure how to ask for it. Why would she want to help me?

Andy

Dear Andy,

It's hard to ask for help sometimes, isn't it? I know just what you mean. Here's a trick that makes it easier.

Is there some kind of help you can offer the math whiz in return? Maybe she is great at adding and subtracting but not so great at writing. Good thing you're a great writer! Tell her something positive like, "I loved your idea for an adventure story." Then try, "Would you like some help writing it? I could use some help with math. Maybe I can help you with your story, and you could help me with my math."

It just might work. This is the main idea behind cooperating—you both get something you need or want by helping each other out. Everyone is happy in the end.

Frank

Dear Frank,

My dad reads the paper and grumbles that there is too much violence. He says no one seems to know how to fix problems any other way than to fight about them. He says fighting doesn't really fix anything, anyway. Do people always have to fight?

Mike

Dear Mike,

Your dad sounds like a smart guy. He is thinking about a big, big problem. It sure would be great if everyone would just cooperate instead of fight, wouldn't it?

Some people say that we *do* always have to fight because fighting is natural. My mom says that *disagreements* are natural, but fighting can be stopped. My mom taught me there are better ways to work things out.

I think working things out calmly can be a pretty hard thing to do. It's hard to listen to someone when you really, really disagree! I don't think people always have to fight. I can't do much about all those other people. All I can do is try to cooperate instead of fight. I try to talk things through with friends and even with kids who don't like me much. Usually it works. So, Mike, maybe if we do that, other kids will, too. We'll all cooperate a little more and fight a little less. Peace out!

Frank

Grab a piece of paper and a pencil. Here's a fun little quiz for you about some of the letters you've just read.

1. If your sister bugs you a lot:
     A. call your mom up at work and whine about it.
     B. rent your own apartment.
     C. ask your sister to help work it out with you.

2. If your group project is going badly:
     A. tell your teacher a bear ate your homework.
     B. tell your teacher your dad ate your homework.
     C. get your group together to talk about ways to make things better.

3. Talking during class:
     A. will make your teacher really, really like you.
     B. makes it hard for other kids to learn.
     C. will make your teeth turn blue.

4. When a job seems too big to do alone:
     A. pretend you don't have to do it.
     B. ask for help.
     C. hide under the bed.

5. When you have a cool idea for a big project:
     A. make a list of all the people who could help you get it done.
     B. talk about it a lot, but never get it done.
     C. wait until someone else does it, and say it was all your idea.

6. Riding in the car with your stepbrother:
    A. is a terrible idea.
    B. makes you carsick.
    C. can be fun if you plan ahead.

7. If you don't like the scenery in your school play:
    A. nicely share some ideas about how to make it better.
    B. complain about it constantly.
    C. pout.

8. Asking for help:
    A. is too hard. Give up.
    B. is easier if you offer to help someone else first.
    C. is never cool.

9. Violence is:
    A. always the answer.
    B. something that doesn't happen in the United States.
    C. something that happens all around the world.

10. The best way to work out a problem with someone is to:
    A. listen carefully to the other person's side.
    B. tell the other person she's a big dummy.
    C. yell, "You're wrong!" until the other person stops talking.

Answer Key: 1-C, 2-C, 3-B, 4-B, 5-A, 6-C, 7-A, 8-B, 9-C, 10-A

There are lots of people who are good cooperators. Eleanor Roosevelt is a great example of someone who knows how to cooperate!

Eleanor lived from 1884 until 1962. Her family lived in New York. She married Franklin Roosevelt, who later became president. Eleanor was shy, but she learned to talk to reporters and make speeches. She wanted to help people who did not have enough money or much education. Eleanor found other people who knew how to help and got them all to work together.

Eleanor was known for getting all the right people to the same meeting. One of Eleanor's biggest beliefs was that countries all around the world should meet and talk together so there could be peace. She believed in the United Nations, a group of all the countries working together. She became head of the United Nations Human Rights Commission and wrote a paper on what rights belong to all people of the world.

Eleanor was known for working well with other people. She said you could never have too many friends. She made friends everywhere and helped them learn to work together to get things done. Now that's cooperation!

Glossary

Here's a list of some of my favorite words and expressions from today's letters.

advice–suggestions from people who think they know what you should do about a problem

common ground–another way of saying you've found something that you and someone else agree on

considerate–being polite, having good manners, and being thoughtful of other people

cooperation–working together; you can make really good things happen this way

disagreement–when you have a different opinion than someone else, you may argue or disagree; this is a disagreement

violence–hurting someone else with words or actions; yelling bad words and hitting are both violent actions

To Learn More

At the Library

Lalli, Judy. *I Like Being Me: Poems for Children About Feeling Special, Appreciating Others, and Getting Along.* Minneapolis: Free Spirit, 1997.

Teitelbaum, Michael. *Working Together.* New York: Scholastic, 2001.

Whitney, Brooks. *Oh, Brother…Oh, Sister! A Sister's Guide to Getting Along.* Middleton, Wis.: American Girl, 1999.

On the Web

FactHound offers a safe, fun way to find Web sites related to this book. All of the sites on FactHound have been researched by our staff. *www.facthound.com*

1. Visit the FactHound home page.
2. Enter a search word related to this book, or type in this special code: 1404806210.
3. Click on the FETCH IT button.

Your trusty FactHound will fetch the best Web sites for you!

Index

Books in This Series

- **Do I Have To? Kids Talk About Responsibility**

- **How Could You? Kids Talk About Trust**

- **I Can Do It! Kids Talk About Courage**

- **Is That True? Kids Talk About Honesty**

- **May I Help You? Kids Talk About Caring**

- **No Fair! Kids Talk About Fairness**

- **Pitch In! Kids Talk About Cooperation**

- **Let's Get Along! Kids Talk About Tolerance**

- **Treat Me Right! Kids Talk About Respect**

- **Want to Play? Kids Talk About Friendliness**

- **We Live Here Too! Kids Talk About Good Citizenship**

- **You First! Kids Talk About Consideration**